PLUGGING INTO PASSIONS

HOW TO LEVERAGE MOTIVATORS AT WORK TO MOBILIZE ENERGY FOR CHANGE

MYRON RADIO
AND
WENDY MACK

IUNIVERSE, INC.
BLOOMINGTON

Plugging Into Passions
How to Leverage Motivators at Work to Mobilize Energy for Change

iUniverse books may be ordered through booksellers or by contacting:

iUniverse
1663 Liberty Drive
Bloomington, IN 47403
www.iuniverse.com
1-800-Authors (1-800-288-4677)

ISBN: 978-1-4620-0212-2 (sc)
ISBN: 978-1-4620-0213-9 (ebk)

Printed in the United States of America

iUniverse rev. date: 3/16/2011

DEDICATION

This book is dedicated to our families, friends, colleagues and clients who continue to support us.

CONTENTS

INTRODUCTION: CHANGE LEADERSHIP IS MORE CRUCIAL THAN EVER

Whether you are a director, vice-president, functional leader, or program or project lead, one of the most powerful and pivotal roles you can play in your organization is that of a change leader. Markets change, technologies evolve, the competition shifts, and mergers and acquisitions occur. As a result, your organization must constantly change in order to succeed and survive. And it is your job to lead the transformation.

WILL YOU RISE TO THE CHALLENGE?

Many of the leaders we've met report that their proudest accomplishments revolve around a time that they led a change successfully and accomplished it through a total team effort. In their bestselling book, *The Leadership Challenge*, Jim Kouzes and Barry Posner suggest that the study of leadership is in fact "the study of how men and women guide us through adversity, uncertainty, hardship, disruption, transformation, and transition."[1] In other words, leadership is all about change and change requires leadership.

> Many leaders report that their proudest accomplishments revolve around a time that they led a change successfully.

The Challenge of Being a Change Leader

You know that changing will help your organization gain a competitive advantage, enter new markets, improve the productivity and effectiveness of your workforce, and so on. Yet, when your employees and stakeholders hear about a new change effort, most will shudder and roll their eyes. In fact, when we interviewed leaders about change efforts, they repeatedly cited resistance as the primary obstacle to transformation. These leaders were often surprised and perplexed by people's reactions to change. Yet most change efforts reportedly fail precisely because leaders fail to take the human side of transition into account.

Introducing Plugging into Passions: A Process for Motivating and Mobilizing People

Plugging into Passions is a process for leading change that focuses on the individuals at every level of your organization. The process merges overall best practices in change management with recent developments in assessment methodologies to provide a powerful new approach for leaders at all levels.

> Plugging into Passions is a process for leading change that focuses on the individuals at every level of your organization.

Thanks to these new developments, we can actually predict with great certainty how individuals will react and adapt to change. By being able to predict those reactions, leaders can create implementation strategies that not only reduce resistance, but that actually create a firestorm of support.

Plugging into Passions is grounded in the belief that the most effective way to get people to embrace and accelerate change is to unleash the energy that is at the core of each person. It is not a magic bullet, but it is a crucial tool for anyone who strives to be an effective change leader.

CHAPTER 1:
INTRODUCING INTERNAL ENERGY

THE CONNECTION BETWEEN ENERGY AND CHANGE

Organization researchers are discovering what you may already know intuitively—energy plays a critical role in individual, team, and organizational performance. As leadership expert Richard Neslund puts it, "Energy is the fuel that powers the engines of performance."[2]

When it comes to leading change, energy becomes even more imperative. In 2008, the global management consulting firm McKinsey & Company surveyed 1,500 executives about transformation projects. McKinsey found that the companies whose change efforts were successful reported that they had been able to sustain and mobilize organizational energy during the transformation. The same survey showed that more than half of the companies with failed change efforts reported that they were unsuccessful at mobilizing and sustaining energy.[3]

> All change requires energy. The key to leading change starts with your ability to energize others.

HOW DO YOU GENERATE ENERGY?

Being an energizing leader is not about delivering motivational speeches and holding pizza parties at work. While the ability to inspire is important, effective leaders recognize that being an energizer is not

1

about "projecting" energy as much as it about uncovering and unleashing energy to achieve a specific result.

SOURCES OF ENERGY

So where does energy come from? Through our research and hands-on experience with clients, we discovered that there are four sources of energy at work inside organizations:

1. Internal Energy

2. Interpersonal Energy

3. Group Energy

4. Organizational Energy

ORGANIZATIONAL ENERGY

Much of the literature available on leading and communicating change focuses on organizational energy. Organizational energy occurs when employees at all levels share a sense of urgency, a clear sense of direction, a commitment to action, and empowerment.

Of course no one would deny that change is more successful when there is organizational energy. Unfortunately, too many leaders rely on the wrong methods in their attempts to reach this point. They want to hold town hall meetings that energize 20,000 people in one fell swoop. What typically ends up happening is that people feel a temporary surge during a meeting like this, but not enough individual commitment to implement lasting changes in behavior. We have found that organizational energy is truly achieved only when corporate and mass communication methods are combined with the actions of individual leaders who leverage internal, interpersonal, and group energy.

INTERPERSONAL AND GROUP ENERGY

Group and interpersonal energy are closely linked. Interpersonal energy comes from the interactions that take place between individual employees and their colleagues and managers. When interpersonal energy is combined with the fundamentals of good management (a clear purpose, effective processes, conflict resolution, and removal of barriers) the result is group energy.

> Interpersonal energy combined with good
> management results in group energy.

Interpersonal energy requires each person to be able to contribute meaningfully. It also arises as a result of a compelling vision. Two key factors in group energy are an igniting purpose and cooperative mindsets. A crucial perspective of this book is that all of these elements—meaningful contribution, compelling vision, igniting purpose, and mindset—are, in fact, highly personal.

Making a meaningful contribution may mean something different for you than it does for your colleague next door. A vision might be compelling for one person yet remain unconvincing to another person. The purpose that ignites me may do little to motivate you.

Without a doubt, interpersonal and group energy are crucial for successful change. Yet again though, neither can be achieved without first attending to the most personal and powerful aspect of energy—internal energy.

To create the energy for change, we need to be able to tap into the highly personal and unique internal energy at the core of each and every person.

INTERNAL ENERGY

This book focuses on internal energy for two reasons. First, no change takes place without individual changes in behavior. For your change effort to be a success, you need each person on your team to be motivated to take proactive steps to do something differently. They need to be energized enough to overcome inertia, habits, and the status quo. As management consultant Connie Hritz says, "If you've lived through change, you already know that it occurs one person at a time … so focus your change management efforts on getting individual commitment."[4]

Second, we have discovered that internal energy is a powerful source of motivation. Tapping into a person's internal energy is like tapping into a gusher of oil. When you understand what drives each person on your team, your job becomes easy. You don't need to micromanage your team—you unleash and channel your team members' energy and get out of the way!

Internal energy is the most powerful source of motivation.

CHAPTER 2:
UNDERSTANDING
INTERNAL ENERGY

This chapter covers a key element of internal energy that we call Passion. Before you read on, reflect on these questions.

- What do the words "motivation" and "energized" mean to you?

- How do you recognize when someone is motivated and energized?

- Would knowing someone's motivation be important to you?

> What if you had a way to identify what motivates
> your employees, peers, boss, and stakeholders?

MOTIVATION MAGIC

Employee motivation is a perennial hot topic for leaders at all levels. Hundreds of thousands of books on motivational methods and tools are purchased every year. Advice on motivation covers topics ranging from the design of pay systems to creating a great place to work to giving people time off. None of this advice is wrong, but none of it is right either. Motivation is highly personal and largely internal. What matters to one person may mean nothing to his or her colleagues.

What if you had a way to identify what motivates each person on your team? What if your conversations with each employee could be tailored to emphasize what matters most to him or her? What if you could match each person's tasks and overall responsibilities to his or her strengths? You can do all of this if you understand internal energy.

Assessing Passions

In our work with teams over the past three decades, we have utilized a variety of assessment tools that measure people's preferred behavior style. These assessments allow observers to place people into several different categories in an effort to explain and predict their behaviors or actions. Over time, we added an additional assessment to our portfolio to enable us to identify the motivations that energize us and in turn drive our behavior.

Research in the area of measuring a person's motivation and values dates back to the work of the German psychologist, teacher, and philosopher Eduard Spranger and his 1928 publication, "Types of Men." Spranger proposed that there are six basic types of attitudes. While all six attitudes may be present in each of us, our top two really move us to action. His belief was that these attitudes were predetermined, so people should learn to understand them and be who they are.[5] Bill Bonnstetter further defined Spranger's seminal work over the years. Bonnstetter developed the first sophisticated assessment tool based on the six attitudes of Spranger in 1990. In later years, he refined the instrument for use in business settings and created the Workplace Motivators (WPM) assessment.[6] We now use the WPM to assess one's passions, motivations, or values in the workplace.

For the first time, we are able to map a person's work activities to his/her energy patterns and leverage resources across the team for greater joint success. Imagine the impact this can have on the productivity of your workforce!

THE SIX PASSIONS

Passion is the term we use to describe what moves and motivates us to take action. Our passion reflects our inner feelings and motivations. Researchers have identified six culture-neutral, gender-neutral core motivators.

- Passion for Knowledge

- Passion for Results

- Passion for Creativity

- Passion for People

- Passion for Leading

- Passion for Tradition

Each of these six passions is present in all of us to differing extents. The real power lies in being able to identify each person's top one or two passions. This will enable us to understand WHY a person will move toward one thing (an event, a project, a work assignment, a group or team, etc.) and away from another.

PASSIONS AND THE POWER OF WHY

In his book, *Start With Why*, Simon Sinek outlines his belief in why some people and organizations are more innovative, more influential and more profitable than others. His examples include the likes of Martin Luther King, Jr., John F Kennedy, Steve Jobs, Sam Walton and the Wright Brothers who fueled their success by understanding their own unique and individual "why". He states, "Those who start with WHY never manipulate, they inspire. And people follow them not because they have to; they follow because they want to."[7]

He also talks about a myriad of companies that started with "why" in their pioneer days, but over time, lost their focus only to become a "me too" within their industry. Essentially, they lost the magic to sustain their momentum and propel their future growth and development.

In *Bury My Heart At Conference Room B*, Stan Slap follows a similar vein. In his no nonsense and often irreverent style he proclaims, "You will never really work for your company until your company really works for you." [8] He links the level of organizational success directly to one's personal value system. Slap asserts that doing so builds "emotional commitment" to the organization at the deepest personal level. He states that "Emotional commitment is the biggest thing a human being has to give; it's unconditional, often overruling logic or self-preservation."

So what is it that both authors link to both personal and organizational success? It's that the ability to tap into your innermost passions and then live and work in a ways that are consistent and congruent with them ultimately lead to self-fulfillment and organizational success. For both authors, passions rule the intellect. They are the keystone that is lodged between what we do and how we do it. Without this keystone, success is a fleeting wish.

Understanding our own passions, and those of others, is therefore helpful in leading change, selecting team members, making assignments, and communicating with others.

Read more about each passion on the following pages—first to understand your own personal passions and then to form some educated guesses about the passions of your team members and colleagues.

PASSION FOR KNOWLEDGE

The Theoretical Motivator

People with a passion for knowledge have a distinct intellectual curiosity. They need to understand how things work and why they work the way they do. These people are generally considered by others to be intellectual. They are eager learners interested in new methods and how they can be applied to existing situations. As continuous lifelong learners, they are objective and nonjudgmental. They like to use their knowledge to be the expert in their chosen field.

Key Words and Phrases: Learn, Understand, Curious, Know, Deeper Meaning, Smart, Wise, Intelligent, Analyze, etc.

PASSION FOR RESULTS

The Utilitarian Motivator

Those with a passion for results value personal and organizational accomplishments. They are naturally drawn to work that allows them to have a bottom-line impact. These folks are pragmatic, practical, and adept at doing just what is necessary to achieve the business result. They are resourceful at optimizing the physical, financial, and human resources available to them. They like to be rewarded through a combination of financial means, recognition, career opportunities, and other areas of perceived value in exchange for their investment of time, energy, and resources to the enterprise.

Key Words and Phrases: Practical, Productive, Return on Investment (ROI), Useful, Earn, Invest, Achieve, Bottom Line, etc.

PASSION FOR CREATIVITY

The Aesthetic Motivator

People with a passion for creativity have a personal value for self-expression. They may be creative in the artistic sense with a keen interest in the fine arts (music, dance, art) or in some other creative activity (photography, crafts, writing, etc.). In the work environment, these people can be very creative, imaginative, and innovative in developing and portraying new products and services. They also strive to maintain harmony in their work environment and in their work-life balance. These folks do need some solitary time for reflection and re-balancing their work lives.

Key Words and Phrases: Create, Harmony, Balance, Appreciate, Work/Life Balance, Time to Reenergize, etc.

PASSION FOR PEOPLE

The Social Motivator

People with a passion for people are altruistic. They value opportunities to serve others and to contribute to the higher good of their groups, teams, families, or organizations. These folks are often called humanitarians. They have a strong drive to help others learn and grow. At work, these people freely volunteer to help others. They make good teachers, coaches, and mentors. They are strong team players and will often put others before themselves. They may also find themselves attracted to not-for-profit organizations and/or caregiver roles.

Key Words and Phrases: Help You, Serve, Contribute, Teach, Coach, Humanity, Connect, Volunteer, People, etc.

PASSION FOR LEADING

The Individualistic Motivator

People with a passion for leading have a strong drive to express their personal power. They like to be seen as unique and distinctive and as the "go to" person in times of crisis. As leaders of the pack, they work very hard to be #1. They are assertive, determined, adaptable, and spontaneous in work that gives them a sense of "standing" and respect in the eyes of others. They are quick to recover from adversity. They like to be positioned in a niche where they can excel and stand out in the marketplace. When the going gets tough, these people naturally rise to the occasion.

Key Words and Phrases: Lead, Be #1, The Best, Energetic, Distinctive, Excel, Power, Succeed, etc.

PASSION FOR TRADITION

The Traditional Motivator

People with a passion for tradition uphold values, rules, and regulations. They are the standard bearers of traditional organizations and can be seen as the guardians of the corporate culture. They are structured, orderly, and precise in their approaches to their work and to their lives. They work extremely well with others who share their high standards and values. They will often sacrifice themselves for a cause.

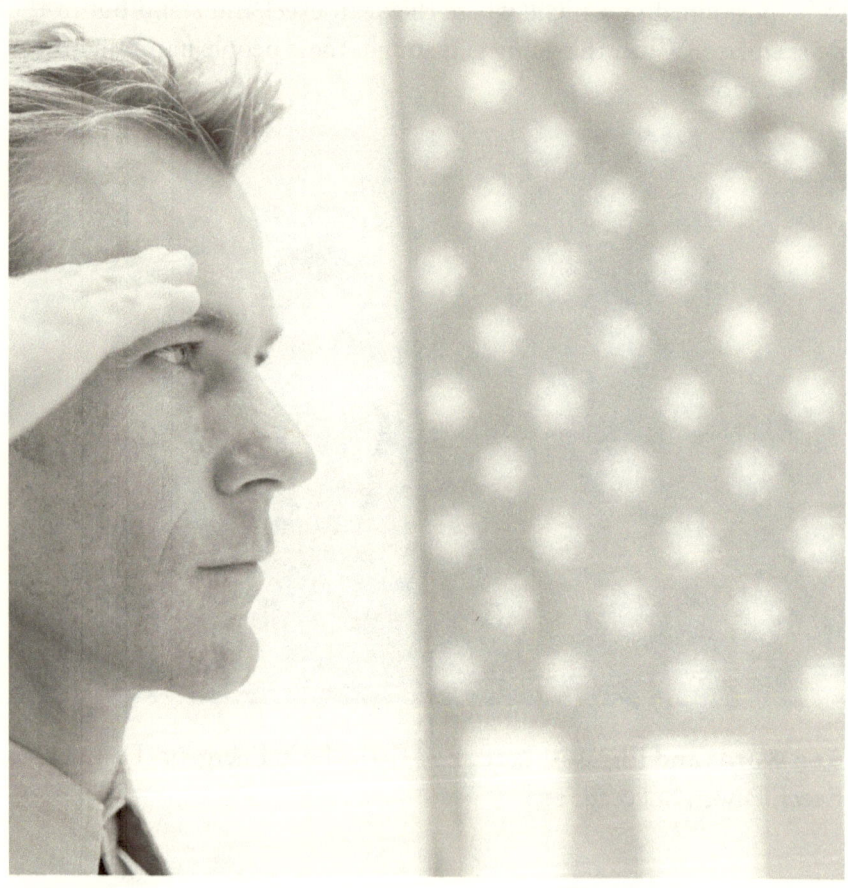

Key Words and Phrases: Standards, Discipline, Protocol, Chain of Command, Stability, Beliefs, Routines, Sacrifice, etc.

Once we understand someone's passion hierarchy, we are able to explain their internal decision-making criteria. Passions capture what we value. When we have to make a choice, our passions dictate our choices, even when we aren't consciously aware of it.

EXAMPLE

Ed was tasked with evaluating and redesigning his company's leadership training programs. He couldn't wait to get started. He bought or borrowed every book ever written on the topics of leadership and leadership development. He spent six months developing an instrument to gather input from leaders about their own training needs. When the data came in, Ed took another four months to analyze the input and integrate it with what he'd learned from the literature. With two months left in the calendar year, Ed was hard at work developing a model that would integrate all of the possible training programs that the company could offer. Not a single course had been designed or piloted. Ed was shocked when his manager exploded and demanded that the entire new curriculum be ready by the end of the year.

What Ed's manager didn't realize is that Ed has a passion for knowledge. He was highly energized by learning and developing theories and he had been happy during all of those months that the manager felt were wasted. If Ed and his manager had understood each other's motivations (passions) and had been able to talk about one another's priorities, they may have been come up with an approach that was both rigorous and that resulted in a faster redesign.

What if Ed's manager had recognized that Ed was energized by learning while he himself was energized by producing results? They could have explicitly discussed ways to satisfy both passions. Perhaps they could have agreed to pilot a new course within the first six months. Maybe Ed could have viewed the pilot as an opportunity to learn.

CHAPTER 3:
LEVERAGING PASSIONS
TO LEAD CHANGE

Because our passions are largely subconscious and because our passions drive our choices and behaviors, they represent the most powerful element of internal energy. Marketers and salespeople have known for decades that success in influencing consumers comes down to being able to connect to what matters to them at a deep level.

While you aren't "selling" per se, a great deal of your success as a change leader will depend on your ability to influence and engage other people. Passions are a powerful tool for doing so. As a change leader, you can use your understanding of passions to:

- Identify people's priorities and motivations

- Recognize what may be behind people's responses to change

- Talk about a change initiative in a way that will motivate people to want to participate

CHANGE REQUIRES COMMITMENT

In our view, leading change is about getting wholehearted commitment— one person at a time. We agree with Thomas Herrington and Patrick Malone, who write, "Wholehearted implies leaders have engaged their followers emotionally and intellectually—both in the heart and head. Wholehearted also implies that the follower decides whether or not to give his or her commitment."[9] So how do you gain wholehearted commitment? You plug into each person's passions.

> Leading change is about getting wholehearted commitment—one person at a time.

PLUGGING INTO PASSIONS

Imagine for a moment that you are able to identify each of your teammates' highest areas of passion or motivation. With this knowledge you could begin to assign people to change initiatives based on where their passion lies. You could also use this insight to shape internal communications to quickly get people committed to the system, process, procedure, and people changes that accompany every major change initiative.

The Plugging into Passions process combines an understanding of energy with the skills of communication and engagement. The four key steps are:

1. Understand each person's internal energy/passions/motivators.

2. Connect and communicate to promote openness to change.

3. Appreciate and address resistance.

4. Unleash each person's energy to power the change.

In the following chapters, you will learn tips, techniques, and suggestions for each of these steps. You will also have the opportunity to learn from the stories of other leaders who have used these skills and techniques.

CAVEATS AND CAUTIONS

Before we go into more detail, however, we want to address a philosophical point.

> Plugging into Passions is something you
> do with people—not to them.

We've seen these four steps in action enough to know what a powerful process it is. Unfortunately there are always a few people in any organization who think that this process will give them a "leg up over others." We want to be clear that plugging into passions is something you do in partnership with others. The idea is not to "psych out" other people or to trick them into accepting a change. We want you and your team to have the words to speak each other's language and the tools to talk openly in a way that energizes everyone involved.

Now that you have seen the steps of the process, let's look at the specifics of how to implement them. The next four chapters are devoted to each of the four steps.

CHAPTER 4:
UNDERSTANDING EACH
PERSON'S INTERNAL ENERGY

When Plugging into Passions, Step 1 is to understand each of your people's internal energy.

> Step 1: Understand each of your people's internal energy.

In Chapter 2 you learned that every person is driven or energized by two or three main motivators. These motivators include:

- Passion for Knowledge
- Passion for Results
- Passion for Creativity
- Passion for People
- Passion for Leading
- Passion for Tradition

Let's now take these motivators and begin to apply them to your team. Even without an official assessment, you may have been able to form some guesses about the passions of the people you work with. Take a few minutes now to jot down your observations below. If you are not sure, or don't have enough data to come to a conclusion, just leave that section blank. This is simply a tool to help you begin to apply what you are learning.

Tool: Passion Chart

Passion	Clues	Team Members:
Knowledge	• They need to understand how why things work the way they do. • They are eager learners and are interested in applying new methods to existing situations. • They like to use their knowledge to be the expert in their chosen field.	
Results	• They are naturally drawn to work that allows them to have a bottom-line impact. • They are pragmatic and practical. • They like to be rewarded through a combination of financial means, public recognition, and career opportunities.	
Creativity	• They have a personal value for self-expression. • They can be very creative, imaginative, and innovative in developing and portraying new products and services. • They strive to maintain harmony in their work environment.	

Passion	Clues	Team Members:
People	• They value opportunities to serve others and to contribute to the higher good of their groups, teams, families, or organizations. • They have a strong drive to help others learn and grow. • They are strong team players who will often put others before themselves.	
Leading	• They like to be seen as unique and distinctive and the go-to person in times of crisis. • They work very hard to be #1. • They are assertive, determined, and adaptable.	
Tradition	• They uphold traditions, values, and regulations and are often the guardians of corporate culture. • They are structured, orderly, and precise in their approach to their work and to their lives. • They will often sacrifice themselves for a cause.	

Once you have finished, take a look back at your charts. Do you have a lot of question marks? That's not unusual. It can be difficult to come to conclusions without having other means to validate or negate your impression. Having listed your own observations, it is now critical for you to confirm or revise your assumptions.

We strongly suggest that you talk with each of your team members about their internal energy. In particular, you might discover that people's passions/motivators are different than what you initially thought. You may also want to consider asking each of your team members to take the assessment that measures workplace motivators.

With or without the formal assessments, we believe that a general understanding of the concepts is enough to help you and your team members begin to have conversations about what matters most to them and what energizes them. Taking the time to really get to know each person you are working with will make the next steps much easier and will make you a better leader in general.

The next chapters will help you use what you now know about your team members' internal energy to help you connect and communicate in a way that leads to genuine commitment.

> "If there is any one secret of success, it lies in the ability to get the other person's point of view and see things from his angle as well as from your own."
> –Henry Ford

CHAPTER 5:
CONNECTING AND
COMMUNICATING

Once you have identified the elements of energy that are core to each person, your next task is to promote openness to change. How do you this? By connecting with what each person cares about! When you interact with each person, you have the opportunity to connect your message to their own sources of energy.

> Step 2: Connect and communicate to promote openness to change.

CONNECTING WITH PEOPLE BASED ON PASSIONS

As we discussed earlier, our passions indicate what we are drawn toward and what we move away from. Being able to connect with people around the things that energize and motivate them at their deepest subconscious level may mean the difference between indifference, rejection, and wholehearted commitment.

> "The only way on earth to influence the other fellow is to
> talk about what he wants and show him how to get it."
> –Dale Carnegie

In Chapter 2, you read the details of the six passions. As a reminder, the table on the next page summarizes the trigger words for each passion.

Below, you'll see an example of how one leader learned to connect with people's passions.

CONNECTING BASED ON PASSIONS EXAMPLE

When two industry giants merged, integration teams from each of the legacy organizations were chartered to work together to address the concerns of the SEC, which was overseeing the merger. When the two integration teams came together to discuss the SEC requirements, disagreements about how to proceed quickly surfaced.

In our work with the teams, we helped them identify the passions that their organizations had been founded on. It became clear that one of the legacy companies embodied Passion for Results. It was known for being quick to market. The leadership team cherished responsiveness and empowered employees to act quickly. The other equally successful legacy firm had flourished based on a Passion for Tradition. Its employees were slower to act, prided themselves on flawless execution by following the intent of the law, and ran every option up the management chain before finalizing a decision.

Once the teams understood each other's perspective, they were able to combine the best of both organizations to deliver timely and accurate data to gain SEC approval in a smooth and seamless way. In fact, the new chairman said, "Our integration teams performed above and beyond our expectations. It is hard to believe how much they accomplished in such a short timeframe." Passion recognition and alignment made all the difference in this instance.

> Promote openness to change by connecting
> with what each person cares about!

People with a Passion for ...	Are energized by words like ...
Knowledge	Learn, Understand, Curious, Know, Deeper Meaning, Smart, Wise, Analyze
Results	Practical, Productive, ROI, Useful, Earn, Achieve, Invest, Bottom Line
Creativity	Create, Harmony, Balance, Appreciation, Work/Life, Time to Reenergize
People	Help, Serve, Contribute, Teach, Coach, Humanity, Connect, Volunteer, People
Leading	Lead, Be #1, The Best, Energetic, Distinctive, Excel, Power
Tradition	Standards, Discipline, Protocol, Stability, Beliefs, Routines, Sacrifice

CHAPTER 6:
APPRECIATING AND
ADDRESSING RESISTANCE

Now that you have connected and communicated with each person and/or group, you may think your work is done. It's tempting to believe that a great motivational speech or a persuasive conversation are all you need to make people feel committed enough to drive change. In reality, it rarely happens that way.

The initial conversations we discussed in the last chapter were designed to promote openness—not to seal the deal. Now your job is to understand and respond to each person's level of acceptance or resistance.

Step 3: Appreciate and address resistance.

SURFACING RESISTANCE

A great deal has been written about overcoming resistance. We believe that approaching resistance as something that needs to be "overcome" is precisely the wrong thing to do.

As we discussed earlier, many leaders make the mistake of believing that they are driving change. These leaders often get frustrated by the roadblocks and speed bumps they encounter, and they attempt to steamroll right over anyone who resists their change initiative. In reality, overpowering resistance doesn't reduce problems, it simply hides them.

And hidden problems are like time bombs just waiting to explode and destroy all the work that has gone into your change effort.

> Overpowering resistance doesn't reduce
> problems, it simply hides them.

Therefore, we advocate doing everything you can to use your initial conversations (Step 2) to launch more intensive and meaningful conversations that are specifically designed to draw out resistance. When you find out what is not working, what concerns people have, and where the problems may be and when you respect and appreciate what people have to say, you'll find that you are far more likely to generate commitment and solutions.

One way to view resistance is to look at it from the perspective of what people are doing to impede your change. Instead, we view resistance as a helpful clue. The degree of resistance we encounter indicates whether or not we have built support for our change.

As human beings, when we first face ANY change in our lives (new organization, new assignment, new teammate, etc.), our subconscious minds invoke the pleasure/pain principle. We ask ourselves:

- Will this change bring me pleasure or pain?

- Will this change be good for me or bad for me?

- Will this change make me happy or sad?

If we perceive the change as being good for us, it's easy to commit ourselves and our resources to seeing it through. Alternatively, if we see the change as being harmful to us to any degree, our resistance will kick in.

Ultimately what this means for you is that if you are seeing signs of shock, denial, fear, fatigue, uncertainty, or doubt then this is a clue that people are feeling the change will be harmful to them.

> A change that threatens a person's motivation
> is a hard change to accept.

People with a Passion for ...	Feel a sense of loss from ...
Knowledge	No ability to learn Shallow work Nothing to learn—everything is understood
Results	Wasted resources No interest in ROI Seniority-based incentives
Creativity	Lack of harmony Stifled creativity Workaholic environment
People	Self-promotion Non-people focus Downsizing
Leading	One of many Stagnation Micromanaged
Tradition	Freewheeling organization No rules Everyone for him/herself

VALUE DISSONANCE

A great deal of resistance is rooted in distrust. It is highly unlikely that we will generate commitment from people who don't like or trust us. While there are many factors that build and destroy trust, a key component is the alignment of values between two people. As we discussed earlier, there are six primary values (we call them passions) and people vary widely in terms of their prioritization of each. When you share a value/passion with someone, you feel confident that he/she will make the same decisions you would. Therefore you trust that person more.

So does this mean that people never trust those who have passions that are different from their own? No. In these cases, we have found that trust can still be formed as long as both people's actions are still predictable. I may value people and my boss may value results. It is still possible for me to trust my boss because at some level I know I can count on him to make decisions to put results first. So the key here is not to pretend to be someone you are not, or to try to "fake" your style or passion. The best route is to be authentic, honest, and consistent and to take the time to build relationships with others before attempting to engage them in change.

People will have a hard time being motivated to go against their values. A key to addressing resistance is plugging back into people's passions. If you are driven by one passion and someone is resisting because he/she is driven by another, instead of positioning one value (passion) as winning out over another, look for ways to explore alternatives that support both. Invite discussion by using phrases such as:

- How can we stay in the black during this recession (Passion for Results) and avoid laying people off (Passion for People)?

- How can we look for innovative solutions (Passion for Creativity) and remain true to the products our customers have come to rely on (Passion for Tradition)?

PUSH, PULL, OR POWER?

In talking about addressing resistance, we often use the analogy of teaching a child to jump off a diving board for the first time. The child may be standing at the edge, terrified. You could walk up behind him and push him off. Chances are that if you try this, you'll severely damage his trust in you. You could swim beneath him and beg or plead for him to jump off. This approach could take forever and be very frustrating for both of you. Your other alternative is to tap into the child's internal energy to help him find the personal power to commit to the jump and to follow through. Perhaps he wants to be able to play with the big kids. Perhaps he wants you to know he can come to the pool without your supervision. Perhaps he dreams of doing back flips and belly flops. Plugging into what he wants is the only way for him to feel good about this first jump.

Think about it. When you lead change, do you typically try to push or plead? Wouldn't it be incredible to be able to power change instead? That is Plugging into Passions.

32

> "Leadership is leaders inducing followers to act for certain goals that represent the values and the motivations—the wants and needs, the aspirations and expectations—of both leaders and followers. And the genius of leadership lies in the manner in which leaders see and act on their own and their followers' values and motivations."
> –James McGregor Burns, author of *Leadership*

PLUGGING INTO PASSIONS EXAMPLE

A marketing and sales organization was historically growing its net income at a rate of 6 percent a year. Unfortunately, the market indicators showed that a slowdown in its industry and the industries it sold into was about to occur. In a meeting with the CEO of the parent company, employees projected net income to be flat at $75 million in the coming year. They saw this as a stretch objective given the gloomy forecast by the industry experts.

Upon hearing this, the CEO sat up straight in his chair and said, "Seventy-five million! Walking into this room I intended to tell you that a 6 percent growth rate isn't good enough. Within three years I expect you to contribute $200 million in net income to our enterprise." Jaws dropped as the CEO left the room. One person after another asked, "Where did he get that number? Did he pull it out of the air?" The organization stewed for about a month.

The senior executives then called together 200 members from around the world to decide what to do about this $200 million bogey. Based on their previous interactions with this group, the meeting designers guessed that the top three passions for almost every member of the group were Passion for (1) Results, (2) Leading, and (3) Knowledge. With this information, the meeting facilitators designed a three-day workshop. As the group convened, the lead facilitator asked the group, "If we could do one thing to get us closer to the $200 million target, what would that one thing be?" After a dead silence, the facilitator said, "Let me ask this question in a different way: If we could learn what causes growth in our sector [Knowledge] and if we could use this knowledge to develop a world-class business unit [Leading], what would one thing be that we could we do to get closer to the $200 million prize [Results]?"

Surprising as it may seem, one idea slowly surfaced after another. A list of 25 ideas was generated and then culled down to the 10 that could have the most impact. The group was split into sub-teams of 20 volunteers each to begin to work on the idea that they felt (1) the most energy toward; or (2) the one they felt they could positively impact the most. One of the outputs from their work together was a high-level estimate of the dollar impact related to their area of focus. When all was tallied, the organization leaders felt that they could move from $75 million to $125 million within three years. While this was far short of the goal, it gave the group members hope that they could at least move the needle forward.

This organization worked extremely hard and engaged its entire workforce in this initiative. In every internal communication (newsletters, meetings, presentations, updates, conferences, etc.) and in every external publication (annual report, editorials, advertisements, tradeshows, etc.) leaders spoke in terms of their passion for Knowledge, Leading, and Results. The message resonated across the board because it was congruent with the energy they put forth.

The end of the story is this: The organization did NOT achieve the $200 million goal at the end of year three—the goal was actually achieved at the end of year two! Along the way, leaders stumbled into a market that no other division was selling into. As Louis Pasteur once said, "Chance favors the prepared mind."

CHAPTER 7:
UNLEASHING EACH PERSON'S
ENERGY TO POWER CHANGE

The final step in the Plugging into Passions process is to align and unleash each person's energy to power change. For many leaders, this is the most exciting part. Individuals have been engaged and are now committed. When the leader can match responsibilities to energy, amazing progress can be made in a short period of time!

> Step 4: Unleash each person's energy to power change.

By now you are aware that passion is at the very core of internal energy. Our passions drive our actions and determine what motivates and demotivates us. It should therefore come as no surprise that the most powerful way to unleash energy is to plug into a person's passions.

> When you can match responsibilities to energy, amazing
> progress can be made in a short period of time!

The chart on the next page reminds us of the passions that drive each person on our teams and how you can plug into these passions to unleash people's energy for a change initiative.

People with a Passion for …	Are Driven by …	Best Match Assignments
Knowledge	Intellectual curiosity and the need to understand	These people can play a key role in research, benchmarking, analysis of systems, and development projects where a strong knowledge base is required. They are also very good at finding the best processes, procedures, and systems from two merged companies to be integrated into the new enterprise.
Results	ROI and the need to get results	These people are strong at finding ways to gain a competitive advantage. They are especially adept at identifying value propositions for new products and services that may result from a change.
Creativity	Harmony and the need to achieve balance	These people are strong at quickly bringing order to chaos. Since they need harmony in their lives, they will work to creatively get the organization through the change and back to the steady state as soon as possible.
People	The need to help others	These people are strong at focusing on the people impact of the change. They will be sure that no one gets left behind.

| Leading | The need to lead | These people are strong at leading the change effort. They will confidently communicate the vision, mission, and values of the new organization both internally and externally. |
| Tradition | The need to maintain high standards and controls | These people will initially resist a change effort if it negatively impacts their values and standards. However, once committed, these folks will work long and hard to establish and maintain performance standards and corporate values across the enterprise. |

UNLEASHING PASSIONS EXAMPLE

The example below illustrates the way one team deliberately plugged into passions when forming a change team.

A mid-cap organization was in the process of going through an organizational renewal. As part of their integrated effort, employees completed a thorough review of the computer technology that supported their operating, support, and infrastructure needs. After fully defining both their current state and future state needs, the Executive Leadership Team (ELT) chartered a small cross-functional group of four employees to design the computer technology (hardware and software) that would lead the organization into the future. Team members were selected based on their primary and secondary areas of passion.

The initiative team was lead by Larry, a business executive who had Passions for Leading and Results. As a team leader, Larry focused on ensuring that this team determined solutions that would give them standing with their customers, employees, and competitors. Their technological approach also had to increase their market share, be cost effective, and meet the needs of the businesses they supported.

Jackie, a senior computer analyst, was a natural for the team. She was selected for her Passions for Knowledge and Tradition. Jackie prided herself on keeping up with leading-edge technologies. She was part of a vast network of technical experts around the world who communicated continuously about the latest and greatest in the technology arena. Maintaining high standards of operations was another of Jackie's key objectives—driven by her Passion for Tradition.

Phyllis, a sales executive with a penchant for graphic design, brought a Passion for Creativity to the team. Phyllis knew how to draw attention to products and services in the marketplace. The team relied on her to communicate the benefits of their recommendations in a way that showed their applicability both internally with employees and externally with customers and suppliers.

Henry, a financial executive with Passions for Results and People, rounded out the team. Henry was charged with evaluating the various technology scenarios to find the one or ones that would have the greatest impact on the bottom line. As the team moved through implementation, he was also on point for managing the internal communications strategy and training on the new technology to ensure a high adoption rate.

In the team meeting that kicked off this effort, the executive champions from the ELT presented a high-level charter for this initiative, the reasons each member was picked for the team, and the roles and responsibilities of each. They also noted that they would be available for informal guidance reviews and would act as initiative champions for any presentations the team would subsequently make to the ELT.

The energy of this team for the IT initiative was incredibly high simply because each member was selected based on his/her intrinsic passions. They hit the ground running. When unforeseen challenges or roadblocks arose, the team came together to resolve them with a singleness of purpose. Their work product was delivered and implemented on time and 20 percent under budget. Only minor tweaks were needed in the first few weeks after implementation.

> "The needs of the team are best met
> when we meet the needs of individual persons."
> –Max DePree

CHAPTER 8:
GETTING STARTED

Let's recap. So far, you've learned the six main workplace motivators (what we call Passions) and the four major steps for Plugging into Passions:

1. Understand each person's internal energy.

2. Connect and communicate to promote openness to change.

3. Appreciate and address resistance.

4. Unleash each person's energy to power the change.

PLUGGING INTO YOUR OWN PASSIONS

At this point, we are hoping you are eager to start applying the ideas and techniques from this e-book. Before you do, however, remember that change begins with you. Taking the time to assess your passion and motivation is critical before you begin your work with others.

As you learned earlier, your passions are the most powerful force behind your decisions and actions. The very fact that you are reading a book on leading change indicates that you want to succeed. What else do you know about your passions? What are you driven by?

Often we find that the most important mindset to shift is that of the change leader. If, as you read this book and answered the questions on the previous page, you realized that you will need to demonstrate a new approach to leading change, remember to come back to why you are doing this in the first place. Your passions are what keep you motivated!

We encourage you to take a few moments to answer the questions below and to make an action plan for getting yourself in the mindset to lead successfully.

- What are your top two passions?

- What boosts your energy?

- What drains you?

- How do you react to change?

- How do you initiate/lead change?

- How will you develop, adapt, or partner with others to be more effective as a change leader?

EXAMPLE: SHIFTING A MINDSET BY CONNECTING WITH PASSIONS

Bill is a senior leader we worked with recently. For his entire career, Bill's driving style and Passion for Leading were recognized and rewarded by his organization. He surrounded himself with the best and brightest "stars" and he rewarded them accordingly.

A new CEO/president took over Bill's company and quickly decided that there needed to be a significant culture shift. He and the HR organization made plans to change their reward system from recognizing star performance to one that would recognize team performance. Bill openly displayed dissent against this change as "flavor of the month." While he did not explicitly sabotage team efforts, his communications and actions demonstrated an obvious lack of support. Internally, he could not wait until this initiative would pass.

The personal challenge for Bill escalated when the team initiative really took off. Support from both the top and bottom of the organization was so strong that additional team initiatives began to sprout roots. Then one day, Bill's leader came to him. He told Bill that the company was about to undertake a significant change initiative that the executive board felt could really propel them beyond the competition. They named Bill to lead this change effort.

Now Bill had a decision to make. He could no longer fake it. He either had to get on board quickly and lead this change OR exit this bus at the next stop. First, Bill looked inside himself to find his true passions. His Passion for Leading and his Passion for Results became the motivators for his change in mindset and attitude. Bill realized that in order to lead, he would need to become a genuine champion for the new change effort. He also shifted his mindset to focus on getting satisfaction from team results, rather than individual measures. Bill didn't change his passions, he simply learned to connect the organizations priorities and expectations with what mattered to and motivated him.

WHAT NEXT?

Where do you begin when it comes to applying what you've learned with your own team? In our work we have seen leaders successfully apply this process using formal, informal, and hybrid approaches.

THE FORMAL APPROACH

In earlier chapters, you began to form some hypotheses about your team members' internal energy. By nature, the process you used to come to those conclusions is very subjective and dependent on your personal point of view. To get a more accurate picture of a person's internal energy patterns in our practice, we use a series of scientifically based online assessments that are much more accurate and objective. If you'd like to explore using these assessments with your team, we ask you to use the phone or e-mail information on the last page of this book to contact us.

Engaging an outside consultant is an example of the formal approach to implementing the Plugging into Passions approach. In the formal approach, a consultant will partner with you to:

1. Have everyone on your team complete assessments to gauge their passions/motivators.

2. Bring your team together to share assessment results.

3. Help you implement the four steps in partnership with individuals on your team.

4. Bring the team together periodically for energizing interactions that focus on aligning, channeling, and unleashing energy in order to help the team as a whole succeed.

THE INFORMAL APPROACH

While we've been a part of many successful change efforts, there are countless other situations where individual leaders have applied what they have learned about internal energy without our direct and personal help. These leaders use a variety of creative approaches, such as giving a copy of this book to each person on their team and then having "book group" discussions about how the team can apply the concepts to their own change projects. Others apply their own awareness of internal energy to initiate conversations with their people about their strengths and what energizes or de-energizes them—without necessarily using a formal assessment or even the names of the styles and passions.

A HYBRID APPROACH

Lastly, you can experiment with a hybrid approach. In cases like this, you might hire a consultant to help your team understand the concept of internal energy and the six types of motivators/passions. With a shared understanding, you and your team will immediately be able to have meaningful discussions about who can best contribute where and how.

KEY TAKEAWAYS

Whether you choose a formal, informal, or hybrid approach, we hope you will find value in remembering these key points:

- Individual commitment is at the heart of all successful change.

- Commitment is the result of truly connecting, communicating, and collaborating.

Making a meaningful contribution may mean something different for you than it does for your colleague next door. A vision might be compelling for one person yet remain unconvincing to another person. The purpose that ignites me may do little to motivate you. To create the energy for change, we need to be able to tap into the highly personal and unique internal energy at the core of each and every person.

CHAPTER 9:
SUSTAINING CHANGE

At this point you may expect that you should be seeing change all around you. But despite all of your hard work, you aren't done yet.

You may have started a fire, but this is the worst time to abandon your people. After all, you know what they call people who light fires and leave, right? Arsonists!

You can implement the steps we discussed and still not see change taking place. People can be all fired up—and go nowhere.

Think about the last time you flew across the country. Your plane landed and taxied to the gate. The second everyone heard that "ding" and the seat belt light went off, what happened? Everyone on airplane jumped up and went nowhere! They felt the urgency—they wanted to get off that plane—but they couldn't do anything about it.

If you want to see real change happen, you have to empower people to make it happen. Now "empower" is one of those words that can mean a lot of different things to different people. When we use it here, we mean giving people what they need in order to take action. If people don't have what they need or if something is in their way, change is not going to happen!

EMPOWERING YOUR TEAM

Once you have unleashed the energy at the core of your people, you need to ensure that they are empowered to take action. The reality is that we could devote an entire book to this topic alone. For the sake of time, let's look at just a few of the most essential factors:

- Clear expectations

- Access to information

- Authority

- Equipment

- Knowledge, skills, and ability

John Kotter points out that when people are left to fend for themselves, frustration grows and change is undermined.[10] Take a minute or two to think about the changes you'd like to see in your organization. Now put yourself in the shoes of one of your frontline employees. What will he or she need to make that happen? Have you asked?

Reinforcing Change

Ultimately every organizational transformation comes down to changing people's behavior. If you ever raised a pet or a child, then you have experience in changing behavior. Based on your experience, you know that behavior changes don't happen without reinforcement. While the steps you have learned here will help you get started, you also need to be sure to pay attention to reinforcing the change you want to see.

One way to reinforce change is to reconnect with the individuals on your team and your team as a whole. As we discussed earlier, these periodic check-ins not only reinforce change, they can also be key to unleashing interactional and group energy.

> Periodic check-ins not only reinforce change, they can also be key to unleashing interactional and group energy.

A Few Words on Repetition

When you are in the process of leading change, you are going to have to repeat yourself. A lot.

In our work with organizations, we frequently find ourselves reminding clients of this fact. Since they are accountable for getting people committed, they can easily be frustrated when everyone doesn't get it as fast as they want them to.

If you are introducing a new compensation system, reorganizing your company, or introducing a new product, you've probably been working on this long before you unveil it to the people who are going to need to execute the day-to-day details. William Bridges, a renowned expert on organizational transition, calls this phenomenon the Marathon Effect.[11]

If you have ever run (or watched) a large marathon you know that at the start of the event the best runners are right on the starting line. Where are the first-timers? Way at the back! Think about one of the big races with thousands of runners—like the Marine Corp marathon in Washington, D.C. It can take about an hour for someone at the very back to even get up to the start line. By that time, the ones who were at the front are halfway through the race!

If it's your initiative, your project, by the time you say "let's go" you are thinking that everyone should be right there with you on the starting line. They aren't. They are way at the back and they need time to catch up.

Jack Welch reminds us that we have to be patient. He warns that, "The vision becomes boring to the person who came up with it." It's tempting to keep changing your message—making it flashier, making it new. Don't. To get people on the same page, you can't keep giving them new pages.

> When you are in the process of leading change, you are going to have to repeat yourself. A lot.

A FEW WORDS ON REWARDS

Another aspect of reinforcement has to do with rewards. Upton Sinclair once wrote, "It is difficult to get a man to understand something when his salary depends upon his not understanding it." If you want to sustain change, you have to consider what you are paying people to do.

Think about your organization's reward structures—both the informal and the formal. Which behaviors are getting reinforced and rewarded? The new ones you want to see or the old behaviors you want to do away with? If the answer is "the old behaviors," you most likely need to take on a Systems Mindset and involve the right people in revising expectations and reward structures. Remember the old adage: Only behavior that gets rewarded gets repeated.

Of course, when considering rewards, keep in mind intrinsic rewards as well as extrinsic ones. Our awareness of passions has taught us that different people will find various activities to be rewarding or draining. In addition to your organization's formal reward system, you have a powerful tool for change at work in the heart of every person.

FINAL THOUGHTS

Think about the last time you made a campfire. You took steps to prepare the wood and kindling before you lit the match. Once you ignited the spark, you strategically fed fuel to the fire to keep it going.

Organizational change works much the same way. You've got to light a fire inside people, not under them. And you've got to keep feeding the fire if you want it to last.

You've got to connect with people. You've got to understand and address their concerns. You've got to find a way to power change—not push it or plead for it. You've got to close the change gap. We hope Plugging into Passions gives you the tools and techniques to do just that.

> Ultimately, if you want people to change,
> you've got to be the spark that lights the fire within them.

ABOUT THE AUTHORS

Myron J. Radio is the founder and president of The R Group. Myron's specialty is building high-powered teams and developing the people within them. Myron offers a complete range of organizational diagnostics and developmental programs that include meeting facilitation, training, workshops, keynote speeches, and coaching in the areas of change management, strategic and tactical planning, and organizational effectiveness.
mradio@the-r-group.com
(703) 476-5575
www.the-r-group.com

Wendy B. Mack is an expert on leading and communicating change. Since founding T3 Consulting in 2001, Wendy has consulted with dozens of companies on the engagement and communication aspects of their change initiatives. Wendy is also the author of numerous books and articles on the topics of change, communication, and leadership. Wendy works with change leaders and change teams via keynote speeches, workshops, strategic consulting, and coaching.
wendy@wendymack.com
(719) 687-8561
www.wendymack.com

ENDNOTES

1. James Kouzes and Barry Posner, *The Leadership Challenge*, 3rd Edition. (San Francisco: Jossey-Bass, 2002), p 177.

2. Richard Neslund, *Energizing Leadership*, Unpublished Paper, Sept. 2008.

3. "Organizing for Successful Change Management: A McKinsey Global Survey", *The McKinsey Quarterly*, June 2006.

4. Connie Hritz, "Change Model," *Leadership Excellence*, May 2008, p. 14.

5. Eduard Spranger, *Types of Men: The Psychology and Ethics of Personality*. (Halle: Max Niemeyer, 1928). Original work published in 1914.

6. For more information on the Workplace Motivators, see the *Personal Interests, Attitudes and Values Certification and Home Study Guide* by Bill J. Bonnstetter, Randy Jay Widrick and Rick Bowers. Another source is the e-book *If I Knew Then—How to Take Control of Your Career and Build the Lifestyle You Deserve* by Bill J. Bonnstetter.

7. Simon Sinek, *Start With Why*. (Portfolio Hardcover, 2009).

8. Stan Slap, *Bury My Heart At Conference Room B.* (Portfolio Hardcover, 2009). p.20.

9. Thomas Herrington and Patrick Malone, "Cracking the Code", *Leadership Excellence*, Feb. 2008, p.14.

10. John Kotter and Dan Cohen, *The Heart of Change* (Harvard Business School Press, 2002).

11. William Bridges, *Managing Transitions* (Cambridge, MA: Perseus Books, 1991).

www.ingramcontent.com/pod-product-compliance
Lightning Source LLC
Chambersburg PA
CBHW021915170526
45157CB00005B/2080